In

A Collection Of Love Poems

Nevoy A. Cassius

inmyforeverfrance@gmail.com

Contents

Smile

Seeing you makes me smile,

sometimes from ear to ear,

And sometimes I just grin,

Comforted by the thought of you

being near.

Everyday

Yesterday I thought of you,

Today too,

And I'll probably think of you

Tomorrow,

I'm pretty certain I will;

Because although most thought

of mine come n go as quick as a

flash,

The thought of you always

Seems to stick around.

Shine Your Light

When the sun shines we can't
see the stars,
And as much as the stars
would love to be seen in the
day,
The sun can't help the fact
That it is the sun.

Amersham Rd

The sound of your voice makes me
feel at home, and although I have
roamed a thousand miles away
from it, I found myself lost in your
tone;

The sweet rhythms of your words,
wether spoken far or near, wether
blurted out and unprepared or even
enunciated loud and clear,
The music to my ears is your song.
You're all I need to hear;

You keep me in tune with my destiny,

boosting my morale, to the point where

I've become bold enough to face my fears,

Because the warm embrace of your

laughter gave me a sense of security,

I was home sick, and your healing

words became a comfort, and a cure

to me;

Your voice became the beacon of light

that guides weary travelers

through the darkest nights to safe shores

when the tides are high,

Around the rocks of unfamiliar

surroundings, all you need do is cry

out to me and I'll somehow get by;

I've been many places, and seen many

faces unknown,

And only recognized your gaze,

translated through the way that you spoke,

It was the way your voice is accented

In the natural flow of how your words

are pronounced,

And the irony of it all is that you

Showed up unannounced,

And I found myself right back on my

doorstep, filled with confidence and

not an ounce of doubt,

Because I was home.

I Never Told You

I lost count of how many times my
heart skipped a beat,
Or the butterflies that made my
stomach flutter;
Or the times I wanna take your
hand and pull you in close to me,
To let you know that you exist in
a place where there is no other.

I never told you, I felt an instant
connection the first day we met,
And in parting you took a piece of
my soul;
How amazing you are or how
you make me feel blessed,

Cos when I'm broken, all you
need do is smile to make me feel
whole.

I never told you how valuable
you are, and it seems
I never told you because I'm supposed to
keep those kinds feelings and
emotions concealed;
I never told you that you were
mine in my world of make
believe,
I never told you, cos telling you
makes it more real.

I wanna tell you that you're the
girl of my fantasy,
And what I'm saying is, we all
wish for our dreams to come true;

So I'm kind of telling you

in hopes to one day make you

my reality,

But I never told you.

I guess it's something I can't bring

myself to do.

Wow

(Woman Of Wonders)

Wow!

Is the first thought that comes to

mind when I see you. Always

dressed for the occasion no matter

the occasion. Always breathtaking.

It's amazing how you leave me lost

for words, where only the simplest

of phrases will do. Yes, those three

little letters, W-O-W.

I use to sum up my appreciation of

how the style and grace of your

presence, brightens up the most

darkest of days.

To define your elegance.

To give expression to the rush of

excitement I feel the moment
I lay eyes upon your naked body,
and to describe what it feels like to
make love to you, as I get lost in
the wilderness of your untamed,
natural beauty, and drown in your
deep brown eyes.
Wow.
The only expression to use
as I get entangled and trapped by
your alluring sex appeal, that never
fails to captivate me at all times.
To say that you're hot, without
losing my cool.
The best way to let a grown woman
like yourself know when her glow
is stunning, radiant and royale.
How else can I convey this burning
desire I have for you, and what it

all comes down to, in that one brief

single encounter.

Wow!

Nothing else will do.

What else is there to say?

Dry Your Tears

I wanna be the one to dry your tears.
To take the pressures of the world
off your shoulders, when the weight
becomes too much to bare.
The one with whom you share your
inner most brightest, and not so
brightest ideas.
Right there with you, in that moment
of despair,
just when you believed that no one else cared,
Is where I wanna be, to cheer you on,
and to prove to you that you are
even more beautiful when you're at
your most vulnerable and scared,

and because I don't wanna miss that

inevitable day when you shine that little

light, that outshines your peers.

Because you're just better, because you're

different, unusual and rare,

And you are just what I was

searching for, all of these years.

To me your value stretches far beyond

and level of compare,

because compare you to what or who?

Are the questions that leave no clues,

and how unjust and unfair,

when I truly believe that as a one of one you were

born to be revered.

So you should grow to be the person

you'd dare to be, if only you would dare,

Awaken that fearless woman inside of you,

because I know she resides somewhere

deep down in there.

I wanna gaze into her eyes and without

breaking the stare, let her know that she's amazing,

and that she's got what it takes to make it anywhere.

So no matter how far apart we may drift,

I'll always be near,

because you hold a timeless place in my heart,

that for only you I keep spare.

A place to get you ready for the world

when you feel rushed and unprepared,

A place where all your worries just

dissipate and disappear.

And in this place, away from prying eyes

and eavesdropping ears,

you could let down your guard and be at ease

with no need to beware.

Because I wanna be the one to fill you

with enough confidence to let go of

all your fears.

To guide you to spread your wings and

embolden you to feel as though

you can walk on air.

And if a day should come,

when you come back down to earth with a bump,

leaving you feeling a little battered,

bruised and worse for wear.

I wanna be the one to dry your tears,

to repair your broken dream

and give you a reason to persevere.

I Will Follow You

I will follow you to the ends of the earth,
I'd roll the dice and risk it all,
trusting in you when I'm at my lowest,
I will follow you;

Even if you were travelling through
regions where crosses were burning
and the devil was lurking,
Undeterred by the thought, if it implied
we'd reach a destiny where our
future was certain,
My promise would be to never
leave you deserted,
I will follow you;

Through each obstacle without fear,

because you fill my existence with

a greater purpose, driving me to persevere,

But if I should die,

And a higher intellect asked me "Why?"

I'd simply reply, "Because she was

worth it."

Because you are.... completely and utterly worth it.

Missing You

Like a double shot of Jack Daniels

without the Coke, is what missing

you feels like;

Life's good, but you make it

sweeter.

Just Thinking…

Do you like watching sunsets on a

cool summers evening?

Or taking long walks, chatting about

whatever comes to mind?

Do you like to be held by the fire in

the winter season?

Or read a good novel to past the time?

Do you like Monday mornings?

Filled with all the hopes and aspirations

of the week ahead,

Or do you thank God when Friday comes?

And what about free falling,

unaware of where you will end?

Or is making plans more fun?

And what about going to the movies
to watch the latest blockbuster,
with fresh popcorn so buttery and warm?
Or is it better to stay at home
cos the oldies never lose their lustre,
just to see how the greats performed?

Do you like the color red?
Is it a symbol of your most frantic
burning desires?
And what if he acts like a gent,
opens doors and treats you with respect?
Or is it the heat of the moment
that makes your body perspire?

Questions that need answering, like
where do you like to be touched?
Do excuse me if I caught you off guard

but, sometimes I like to be blunt,

And with that said, do you like it rough?

Do you like to wear heels in bed?

Do you like your hair pulled?

Being naughty and spanked on the bum?

Or would you prefer to make love instead?

Do you like to be the object of all

men's obsessions? Driving them crazy at every turn?

Or is having just one man in

your possession. His passion. The one true

pleasure you eternally yearn?

And lastly, do you have an old soul,

that admires the simple things in life,

filled with substance, and never empty and hollow?

Or is youthful exuberance your most

attractive trait,

filled with all the possibilities of tomorrow?

I was just thinking…

I appreciate and thank you for reading 'In My Forever.' All feedback is welcomed as it will be a pleasure to know what you, the readers have to say. I promise to do my absolute best to reply to all your messages so please send your comments and reviews to inmyforeverfrance@gmail.com or alternatively you can leave a book review on my amazon book page.

With love and kind regards,

Nevoy A. Cassius

Printed in Great Britain
by Amazon

73197810R00020